# Guru Nanak
## and
# Sikhism

## Rajinder Singh Panesar

HODDER
*Wayland*

an imprint of Hodder Children's Books

# Great Religious Leaders

The Buddha and Buddhism
Guru Nanak and Sikhism
Krishna and Hinduism

Jesus and Christianity
Muhammad and Islam
Moses and Judaism

 © White-Thomson Publishing Ltd 2002

Produced for Hodder Wayland by White-Thomson Publishing Ltd
2/3 St Andrew's Place, Lewes, E Sussex, BN7 1UP, UK

Editor: Margot Richardson
Designer: Jane Hawkins

Graphics and maps: Tim Mayer
Proofreader: Philippa Smith

First published in 2002 by Hodder Wayland, an imprint of Hodder Children's Books

The right of Rajinder Singh Panesar to be identified as the author of this Work has been asserted by him in accordance with the Copyright, Designs and Patents Act 1988.

British Library Cataloguing in Publication Data
Panesar, Rajinder Singh
  Guru Nanak and Sikhism. - (Great Religious Leaders)
  1. Nanak, Guru 1496-1539  2. Sikhism - Juvenile literature  I. Title
  294.6
ISBN  0 7502 3706 6

Printed in Hong Kong by Wing King Tong Co. Ltd.

Hodder Children's Books
A division of Hodder Headline Limited
338 Euston Road, London NW1 3BH

Cover top: Guru Nanak blessing his followers.

Cover main: The Golden Temple surrounded by its sacred lake.

Title page: Sikh musicians in a gurdwara, England.

Picture Acknowledgements: The publisher would like to thank the following for permission to reproduce their pictures:
AKG 18 (Jean-Louis Nou); Art Directors and Trip Photo Library *cover top*, *title page* (H Rogers), 4 (H Rogers), 8 (H Rogers), 9 (H Rogers), 10 (H Rogers), 11 (H Rogers), 13 (H Rogers), 20 (H Rogers), 21 (H Rogers), 22 (H Rogers), 27 (H Rogers), 32–3 (H Rogers), 33 (H Rogers), 35 (Dinodia), 38 (B Dhanjal), 42 (H Rogers), 43 (H Rogers); Chapel Studios 16 (Zul Mukhida), 19 (Bipin J Mistry), 36 (Zul Mukhida); Chattar Singh Jiwan Singh  6; Circa Photo Library 5 (Bipin J Mistry), 12 (Twin Studio), 14 (John Smith), 23 (Twin Studio), 24 (Twin Studio), 25 (John Smith), 26 (John Smith), 37 (John Smith), 40, 41 (bottom) (John Smith); Eye Ubiquitous *cover main* (Bennett Dean), 15 (David Cumming), 28 (Bennett Dean), 29 (David Cumming), 34 (David Cumming), 39 (Tim Page); IPS Tech Corps/Inderpreet Singh 17; Christine Osborne 30; Rajinder Singh Panesar 31; Hodder Wayland  41 (top), 44, 45 (top and bottom).

# Contents

1   What Is Sikhism?   4

2   The Life of Guru Nanak   6

3   Guru Nanak's Teachings   14

4   The Sikh Scripture   22

5   The Sikhs' Sacred Places   30

6   Festivals and Special Occasions   36

7   Sikhism Today   44

Glossary   46

Further Information   47

Index   48

# What is Sikhism?

Sikhism started in India, in the northern province called Punjab, in the late fifteenth century. Sikhs prefer the term *Sikh Dharam* to Sikhism. It means 'the Sikh way of life'. There are approximately 20,000,000 Sikhs in the world and the vast majority of them live in India, though many of them have now settled throughout the world.

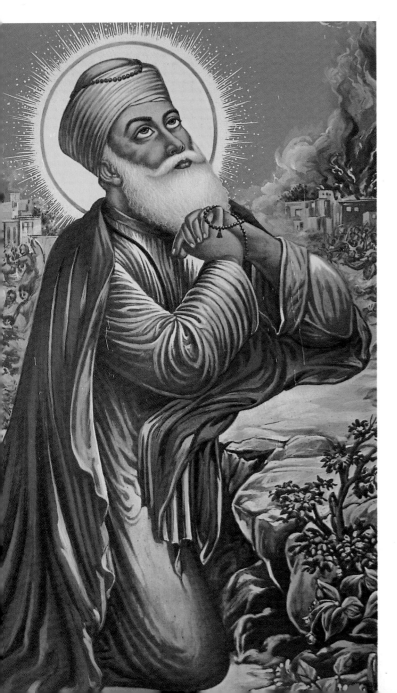

## The founder of Sikhism

Guru Nanak was born in 1469. He was born a Hindu, but Hinduism did not appeal to him. He did not like the worship of many gods, or the Varna system (division of people). He was impressed with the equality of Muslims in Islam, but that equality was only for Muslims. The Guru decided to choose a path of God where everyone is respected as equal, regardless of religion, colour or sex. His instructions were 'there is only one God', or *Ik Onkar* in Punjabi. *Ik Onkar* calls for the blessing of God and forms the first line of the Sikh beliefs, the *Mool Mantar*.

## Sikhs as disciples

The followers of Guru Nanak came to be known as Sikhs. The word 'Sikh' means a disciple or a learner. The word 'Guru' means a teacher. Sikhs use the word Guru for the ten Sikh Gurus and the holy scriptures, *Guru Granth Sahib*.

◀ When Guru Nanak prayed to God, one of the things he asked for was peace in the world.

Sikhism, as started by Guru Nanak and developed by the nine Gurus who followed him, is the simplest way of finding salvation: to escape from wrong-doing and its results. Sikhs must perform their duties to both family and society. They must earn money through honest labour, share food with others (*Langar*), meditate, be charitable and help others (*sewa*).

The *Guru Granth Sahib*, the Sikh holy book, contains the divine hymns of Guru Nanak and the nine Gurus who followed him, along with hymns from many Hindu and Muslim holy men.

## KHANDA: SYMBOL OF SIKHISM

The double-edged sword in the centre represents the authority of one God. The two edges stand for freedom and justice. The circle represents the unbroken bond of a Sikh with God and at the same time shows there is no beginning and end of God, who is infinite. The two blades around the side represent worldly and spiritual freedom. The *Khanda* appears on the Sikh flag which flies outside every Sikh gurdwara (place of worship).

A Sikh couple pose proudly with their daughter. ▼

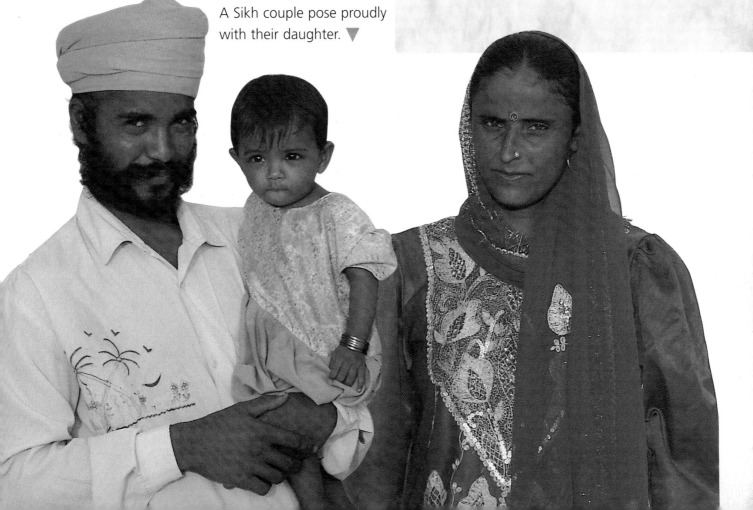

# The Life of Guru Nanak

## Birth of the Great Guru

In the small town of Talwandi lived a man called Mheta Kalu along with his wife, Tripta, and his daughter, Nanaki. Kalu was a respected tax collector for the governor. Late one night he was walking up and down in his garden, looking very worried because his wife was about to give birth to a baby.

Soon he was called by a nurse, called Daultan, who had come to help his wife. She said, 'Sir, congratulations! Your wife has given a birth to a son!'

'But I haven't heard a child cry,' replied Kalu.

'I know. I saw a strange light when he was born, and instead of crying he smiled at me. I think he is going to be someone special,' said Daultan.

This made Kalu so happy that he gave her a gift of money and said, 'Thank you Daultan, and thank you God.'

When Nanak was born, everyone in the town came to congratulate his family. ▼

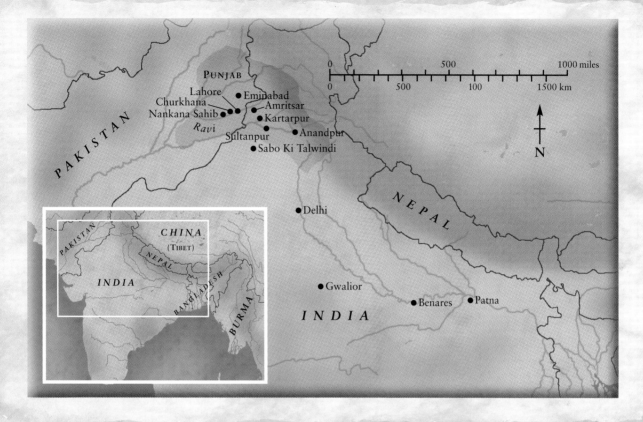

Kalu rushed to the room where his wife lay and was very pleased to see Nanaki holding her brother very proudly. Soon everyone in Talwandi knew about the birth and came to congratulate Kalu. Everyone was given sweets.

A few days later an astrologer called Hardyal Dass was invited to prepare a horoscope for Kalu's son. As the horoscope was completed Hardyal Dass said, 'Sir, your son will be a great leader and many people will love and respect him'. The child was then named Nanak, meaning 'unique one'.

Later, the name of the village was changed to Nankana Sahib meaning 'a place where Nanak came'. This place is now in present-day Pakistan and is a few kilometres from the city of Lahore.

Bhai Gurdass, a Sikh scholar, wrote this hymn in praise of Guru Nanak.

'The merciful God has heard the cries of humanity and sent Guru Nanak to this world. Guru established the religion and brought all four castes together. He treated prince and pauper alike and his followers learned to bow humbly to each other. He performed this great act to show his disciples how to be humble and respectful. ... Guru Nanak came to this world for the redemption of mankind.'

## The Real Bargain

Nanak grew up to become a fine young man, but he was more interested in spending time with monks and learned people than doing any work. Kalu was really worried about Nanak's future, because if Nanak did not work, how could he support himself and a family?

One day Kalu had an idea. He called Nanak and said, 'Nanak, my dear son, here are twenty rupees. Take them, go to the city, buy some goods and sell them at a profit. This way you will be able to earn your living.' Reluctantly, Nanak agreed and took the money. He started his journey with his friend Bala. On the way to the city Nanak saw some monks sitting under a tree. Nanak went over to them and saw that their faces were pale and they looked frail.

Nanak asked, 'Oh holy men, why do you look so unhappy?'

They replied, 'We have been hungry for three days.'

Nanak said to the monks, 'Please wait for a little while longer. I will be back.'

◀ A poster showing stories from Nanak's childhood.
Top left: Guru Nanak at school.
Top right: A deadly cobra shades Guru Nanak from the sun.
Bottom left: Talking to a farmer.
Bottom right: Guru Nanak feeding the hungry monks.

Nanak went into the city, but instead of buying goods to sell he bought food for the monks and took it back to them. The monks were very pleased. They blessed Nanak and said, 'Oh Nanak, God will bless you and your name will shine in the world.' The monks then continued on their journey towards the holy city of Benares.

Now it was Nanak's turn to be sad because he had to face his angry father. On his return, his father told him off but Nanak said, 'What could be a better bargain than feeding the hungry?' This made Kalu even angrier and he was about to hit Nanak, but his sister, Nanaki, saved him from punishment.

Nanaki knew that her brother and father could never get on well. So she asked Kalu if Nanak could move to Sultanpur, where she lived with her husband. Kalu agreed and Nanak moved to his sister's home.

## GURU NANAK AT SULTANPUR

Nanak started his first job as a storekeeper at Sultanpur. He revealed the *Mool Mantar* (the Sikh basic belief) to a gathering in a village. People liked the way Nanak explained how to love and follow God. Some began to call him a 'Guru'; others 'Sat Guru' ('true Guru'). Nanak started his first journey from Sultanpur to spread his teaching to other parts of India.

▲ Guru Nanak leaving Sultanpur on the first of his four great journeys.

▲ A wall painting of Guru Nanak with Lalo at Eminabad. The Guru visited Lalo on the first and third of his great journeys (see page 12).

## Earn an Honest Living

One day, Guru Nanak along with his followers, Bala and Mardana, arrived at a village called Eminabad. The Guru stopped outside a hut and knocked on the door. A poor man called Lalo answered the door and invited them in. He hurriedly spread a mat on the floor and apologized for having no table or chairs. 'That is no problem. We feel comfortable sitting on the floor,' replied the Guru. Lalo offered them some refreshments, which his guests enjoyed.

In the same village lived a rich banker named Malik Bhago. He was a mean and proud person. He was holding a feast to show off his riches. Knowing Nanak was in the village, he invited him too. At first Guru Nanak refused but when Malik asked again the Guru accepted. On the Guru's arrival, Malik asked rudely, 'What was so good about that poor man's hut that you refused to come to my mansion?'

'I love every one equally,' replied the Guru.

When everyone started to eat, the Guru took a piece of bread from the poor man's house in one hand and another piece of bread, from Malik Bhago's table, in his other hand. The Guru squeezed both his hands. Drops of milk came out of the poor man's bread and blood oozed out of the rich man's bread.

'What is this magic?' cried Malik Bhago.

'This is no magic, Malik Bhago. This is the truth,' Guru Nanak announced. 'Since the poor man has earned his food by honest means the milk came from his humble food. But you have used harsh methods to get your food and treated your servants and tenants cruelly. The blood dripped from your bread due to your wickedness and greed.'

Malik Bhago understood the message and begged for forgiveness.

'Be kind to your workers. The blessings of the needy will help you to go to heaven,' said Guru Nanak.

Malik Bhago changed his ways and earned the love and respect of all the villagers.

*'Blessed and beautiful is the hut where God's praise is sung. Worthless is the palace where God is forgotten. Poverty is bliss if it helps to remember God. Having a contented heart is better than ruling a kingdom.'*

*Guru Granth Sahib 745*

◄ Guru Nanak squeezed the bread to prove his point that an honestly earned living is like drinking milk but a dishonestly earned living is like drinking blood.

## The Last Journey

Guru Nanak spent the next twenty years making four long journeys to spread his message of love. He travelled to many countries. Finally, Guru Nanak settled on the banks of the river Ravi, in the village of Kartarpur which he had founded a few years earlier. He had built a small shrine where everyone would gather and pray together. The village people followed Guru Nanak to the fields, and would work hard alongside him during the day. In the evening they assembled at the shrine to listen to the Guru. Everyone cooked in the same kitchen and ate together, regardless of class or creed.

▲ Guru Nanak told everyone that Lahna was to be the next Guru. Each of the ten Gurus chose the following Guru in a similar way.

One day when his life was coming to an end, the Guru called one of his disciples, Lahna. To everyone's amazement he placed five coins and a coconut in front of him. These were a symbol of respect. The Guru said, 'Bhai Lahna, from today you are the Guru of the Sikhs and I name you Angad, meaning "part of my Body".' All the Guru's followers were instructed to follow Angad. Several days later, Guru Nanak died.

It is written that upon the death of Nanak both Hindus and Muslims were arguing among themselves as to whom should perform the final rites. The body of Guru Nanak was lying under a sheet. The Hindus claimed that Nanak was born a Hindu and that he should be cremated. On the other hand, the Muslims said that Nanak was their holy man and a Muslim, therefore they were going to bury him. A wise man appeared and asked why they were fighting. They explained

## THE TEN GURUS

The word guru is from the Sanskrit language.
'gu' means darkness and 'ru' means light. The
word therefore means enlightener or teacher.
In Sikhism, there was only one Guru at any
one time. The ten Gurus were:

|    |                    | Born–Died |
|----|--------------------|-----------|
| 1  | Guru Nanak         | 1469–1539 |
| 2  | Guru Angad         | 1504–1552 |
| 3  | Guru Amar Dass     | 1479–1574 |
| 4  | Guru Ram Dass      | 1534–1581 |
| 5  | Guru Arjan         | 1563–1606 |
| 6  | Guru Har Gobind    | 1595–1644 |
| 7  | Guru Har Rai       | 1630–1661 |
| 8  | Guru Har Krishan   | 1656–1664 |
| 9  | Guru Tegh Bahadur  | 1621–1675 |
| 10 | Guru Gobind Singh  | 1666–1708 |

The Tenth Guru told the Sikhs that there
would be no more human Gurus after him,
but that the *Guru Granth Sahib*, the Sikh
holy book, would be Guru forever.

▲ A poster showing the ten Sikh Gurus.

the situation and, after listening to both sides, he asked them,
  'Have you checked what is underneath the sheet?'
  'No,' they replied. When they looked under the sheet there was no
body but a few flowers. When they turned around there was no wise
man. They realized it was Nanak himself who had come to tell them not
to quarrel. The flowers and the sheet were divided into two halves. The
Hindus cremated their half and the Muslims buried theirs.

# Guru Nanak's Teachings

Guru Nanak laid down three basic rules:
1 *Naam Japna*: meditate
2 *Kirat karna*: earn an honest living
3 *Vand chhakna*: share earnings with needy people.

▲ A painting showing a famous holy man, Puran Singh, doing *sewa* (voluntary work). He is taking a sick man to a Sikh hospital on a bicycle rickshaw.

## Being good to others

Sikhs were instructed to give 10 per cent of their income to good causes. Guru said, 'You must spend 10 per cent of your time in praying and 10 per cent of your time in doing *sewa* (voluntary work).'

Guru Nanak said that the world is like a mirror. It is up to you how you reflect in it. So if you are good to others they will be good to you, and if you are nasty to others you will get the same rudeness back. He also asked Sikhs to believe in one God, the creator of all, and not to believe in or worship many different gods.

## Life after death

The Guru believed that there is a life after death. One's soul never dies; it just keeps moving on to different bodies until it finds a union with God. This is called transmigration.

He explained that when we came into the world we were not able to dress ourselves and when we leave the world we will not be able to dress ourselves either. Whatever we claim as ours does not belong to us. When we die we will even have to leave behind our body. He also explained that God will not judge people by the colour of their skin nor by their religion – but by their actions or deeds.

## The five evils

Guru Nanak taught that there are five evils which control everyone's mind: lust, anger, greed, attachment to worldly wants and ego. If a person can learn to control these then they will always win in life.

### TWO TYPES OF PEOPLE

Guru Nanak said that people could be divided into two groups:

*Manmukh*: a self-centred person, who follows his/her own instinct. Their life is controlled by the five evils mentioned above.

*Gurmukh*: someone who follows the instructions of God. *Gurmukh* has five virtues: truth, patience, contentment, humility and the ability to serve others.

A holy man; someone who follows the instructions of God. He is holding a spear, a weapon used by Sikhs in the past. ▶

# The Status of Women in Sikhism

For many years before Guru Nanak's time, women in India did not have the same status as men. They were treated as slaves. Many called them *Paran di jutee*, meaning 'shoes'. Some parents would kill a girl as soon as she was born. Education was only for men because it was thought that a woman's job was only to look after the house and rear the children.

## 'Half the body'

Guru Nanak was the first to speak against this cruelty. He instructed his followers to call their wives *ardhangnee* meaning 'half the body'; that no man is complete without a woman. He said, 'How can you say bad things about the personality that has given birth to the king of kings?' In Sikhism women have every right to be treated as equals to men. The wives of the Gurus played an active part in helping the Gurus with their preaching. The Guru asked women not to wear a veil to cover their faces but to be proud to work alongside men.

A woman reading the *Guru Granth Sahib*. Women often lead worship in the gurdwara. ▶

## Progress for women

The second Guru, Angad, made sure every woman who wanted to learn and to read was given a chance. He held special reading classes for women.

Bhag Kaur became a general after the famous battle, and survived to lead many more armies.

## A WOMAN'S COURAGE

Guru Nanak said that women should not be considered inferior to men. Once, forty Sikhs deserted the Tenth Guru, Guru Gobind Singh, while he was under siege. Bhag Kaur, a brave woman, told them they were wrong to leave the Guru. She then led them back to the battlefield and won the battle. Her courage earned the men their pardon from the Guru.

The third Guru, Amar Dass, appointed many women as high priests who would preach and collect gifts on behalf of the Guru.

Guru Amar Dass made a law against women covering their faces. He also told his followers not to believe in the evil ceremony of *sati*, where a wife had to jump alive into the funeral pyre of her husband. He said that dying for no reason was a sin. He encouraged the remarriage of widows and of divorced women.

All these changes gave women an equal chance and freedom to work alongside men. They could now help their husbands in farms and shops or earn money to feed their family.

## Equality in Sikhism

During the time of Guru Nanak most ordinary people were treated unfairly. The Moguls, who ruled the country, treated everyone other than Muslims as Kaffirs (unbelievers) or as second-class. If non-Muslims wanted to celebrate a festival or meet (in a group of more than two people), they would have to pay a special tax called *jazia*.

## Children of one god

Guru Nanak spoke out very strongly against this. He preached that, good or bad, we are all children of one god. There should be no division on the grounds of profession, religion, colour or sex. The Guru instructed his followers to treat everybody equally. A Sikh must respect and value the beliefs of others, but at the same time he or she must follow the teachings of the Gurus and no one else.

One of the most important beliefs in Sikhism is that everyone should be equal. The turban, a cloth wrapped around the head, is a symbol of faith for both men and women. ▼

## Langar

To fulfil his aim Guru Nanak began the practice of *Langar*. This is a meal where everyone would help to prepare food and then eat it together, all sitting at the same level. The Guru started this because one of the Indian customs at the time was that different groups of people should not eat together. In fact, the third Guru would not see anybody who did not join in the *Langar*. He would not see even Emperor Akbar, the great ruler of India, until he agreed to eat *Langar* with the Sikhs first.

*Langar* became an important part of the Sikh faith. It is served in every gurdwara today, and is open to everyone. To respect the teachings of the Guru and value the faith of others, only vegetarian food is served. This is because people of some other faiths have strict food rules. For example, Muslims can only eat meat that has been killed in a certain way, and Hindus do not eat beef. By serving vegetarian food only, anyone from any faith can join in *Langar*.

▲ Eating *langar* at Amritsar in India.

'God first created light. Then God created all the living creatures and from the Divine light the whole creation sprang. Why then should we divide human creatures into the high and low classes? says Guru Nanak.'

*Guru Granth Sahib* 1349

# Family Way of Life

In India, at the time of Guru Nanak, many men would leave their homes to go away to the forests or the mountains, to be alone and meditate in God's name. They would not see their wives and families, and cut themselves off from other people and society.

Guru Gobind Singh, the tenth Guru, with his four sons. ▼

## Living in a family

Guru Nanak did not approve of this practice. He told his followers to enjoy family life and to bring up their children as good, God-fearing people.

## FAMILY SUPPORT

Sikhs believe that they can have salvation through living their lives within a household. Sikhs believe that one elder is in charge of the household but will value and respect every member of the family. All family members must respect the elder and contribute equally to the family in return. Some modern families may live in different houses, but will still think of themselves as joint families. They will meet each other regularly and stay close to each other. Some members of a family may be far away in other countries, for economic reasons, but often he or she will support the family by sending money from abroad.

▲ A large Sikh family. Guru Nanak said that by living within the family one realizes the true love of God.

In the *Guru Granth Sahib*, Guru Nanak said that a person does not have to go to the forest to find God. A person must look for God within him or herself. People who leave their homes are not carrying out their responsibilities. If living with one's family was thought of as inferior, monks would not knock on the doors of families and seek help.

Guru Nanak said that a person who has married, has looked after their partner well, and has brought up their children up as law-abiding, God-fearing people has truly understood God's way of life. To prove their point all Gurus except the eighth Guru married and had children. (The eighth Guru could not marry because he died at the age of eight.)

# The Sikh Scripture

The Sikh scripture or holy book is called the *Guru Granth Sahib*. It is the revised version of the original *Adi Granth* which was compiled in 1604 by the fifth Guru, Guru Arjan.

▲ Guru Arjan blessing the congregation. He promised Sikhs that he would compile a *Granth* (a big book).

## A genuine holy book

The need for a true holy book was felt when some impostors began to claim their writings as those of Guru Nanak. Sikhs approached the fifth Guru, Guru Arjan, and asked if there was a way they could be sure of the hymns by Guru Nanak. The Guru told them that he was thinking of collecting all the genuine hymns of Guru Nanak and all the other Gurus and putting them into one big book.

A booklet of hymns, called a *Pothi*, written by Guru Nanak, was passed on to Guru Angad, the second Guru. When Amar Dass became the third Guru he received two of these booklets, one written by Guru Nanak and the other by Guru Angad. Amar Dass compiled all the hymns into one *Pothi* and added his own hymns to it. This *Pothi* was then passed to the fourth Guru, Ram Dass, but after his death it fell into the hands of Baba Mohan, the son of the third Guru.

## Obtaining the *Pothi*

Guru Arjan (the fifth Guru) sent a messenger to bring the *Pothi* back, but Baba Mohan would not part with it. Eventually, Guru Arjan decided to go himself. When the Guru arrived at Baba Mohan's house, Baba Mohan refused to see the Guru. So Guru Arjan sat outside the house and sang a hymn praising God. Baba Mohan was so impressed by the hymn he came out personally and invited the Guru inside. Upon hearing that there was a need to create a book of genuine hymns of all the Gurus, Baba Mohan agreed to give the *Pothi* to Guru Arjan saying, 'In fact, you are the true owner of this *Pothi*'. It is written that the Guru had such high respect for the *Pothi*, he walked barefoot back to Amritsar, carrying it on his head.

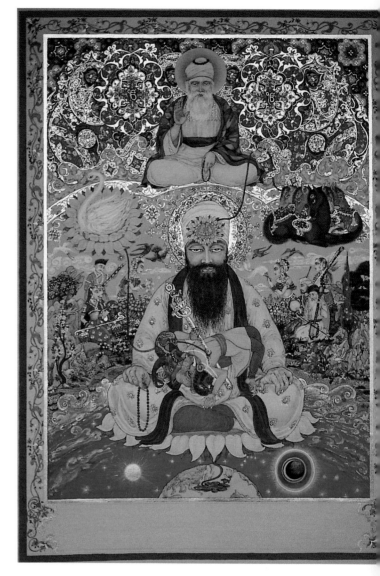

A painting showing that Guru Arjan (below) received spirituality from God through Guru Nanak (above). The five horrible animals in the lap of the Guru represent the five evils a Sikh should conquer. ▶

This is the hymn that Guru Arjan sang outside the house of Baba Mohan:

'O Mohan, your temple is so lofty, and your mansion is unsurpassed.
O Mohan, your gates are so beautiful. They are the worship-houses of the Saints.
In these incomparable worship-houses, they continually sing Kirtan, the Praises of their Lord and Master.
Where the Saints and the Holy gather together, there they meditate on you.
Be Kind and Compassionate, O Merciful Lord; be Merciful to the meek.
Prays Nanak, I thirst for the Blessed Vision of You, receiving Your vision, I am totally at peace.'

Guru Granth Sahib, 248

# Compiling the Scriptures

Work to compile the *Adi Granth* started in August, 1601, and was finally completed in 1604.

Guru Arjan asked the great Sikh scholar, Bhai Gurdass, his mother's brother, to write down the words. It is said that at the gurdwara called Ramsar, which is about 800 metres from the Golden Temple in Amritsar (see page 26), there was once a big tree. Under it sat the Guru and Bhai Gurdass. The Guru dictated the hymns from the previous *Pothi*, while Bhai Gurdass wrote them down. This was a very slow process, as Guru Arjan wanted to make sure that the original hymns composed by the previous Gurus were re-recorded clearly.

Once the hymns of the first three Gurus were re-recorded, the hymns of the fourth Guru were checked and written down. Guru Arjan then recorded his own hymns. Finally, he started the hard work of selecting the hymns composed by many other holy men. It was important that these

◀ Guru Arjan reading the first *Adi Granth*. The man behind him is holding a fan made from peacock feathers, called a *Chauri*, to show respect to the Guru.

hymns fitted within the teachings of Guru Nanak. Altogether, the compositions of fifteen holy men were recorded. Two of these were Muslims and some of them were quite lowly men.

## A scripture for everyone

By recording these people's hymns along with those of the Gurus, Guru Arjan sent a message to his followers that everyone is equal in the eyes of God. The main reason for adding these hymns to the *Adi Granth* was that the Guru wanted it to appeal to everyone, no matter what their religion or status. The Guru achieved his aim; it is said that more people embraced Sikhism during his period than any other period before or after him.

The *Adi Granth* was read again by Guru Arjan himself and declared to be the original. It was then despatched to the city of Lahore for binding with a hard cover for protection.

This became the first and the only holy book to be compiled by one of the Gurus and passed to his followers as an original and undisputed copy.

▲ The Sikh scriptures are written in Gurmukhi script. This copy, at Amritsar, was hand written about 200 years ago.

# The Adi Granth at Harmandir Sahib

In the city of Amritsar, Guru Arjan had built a beautiful Sikh shrine and named it *Harmandir Sahib*, meaning 'divine residence of God'. It was built in the middle of a sacred lake with only one bridge connecting it to a gurdwara. Guru Arjan felt happy and relieved because he had fulfilled the mission of Guru Nanak. Sikhs had their own language, Gurmukhi (now known as Punjabi), their own holy shrine and, above all, their own holy scripture.

## Installing the *Adi Granth*

On the 30 August 1604, the *Adi Granth* was taken to *Harmandir Sahib*. It was placed under a special canopy. A small dais (a low platform) called a *Manji* was prepared and the *Adi Granth* was placed on it. It was then covered

The most important room of *Harmandir Sahib*, where the *Adi Granth* was first placed in 1604. ▼

with a beautiful cloth called a *Rumalla*. A fan called a *Chauri* was prepared and waved over the *Adi Granth* in respect. Baba Bhuda Ji was appointed as the first *Granthi* (a high priest who looks after the sacred text).

Everyone bowed to the *Adi Granth* and sat on the floor giving reverence to the scriptures. It is said that Guru Arjan, from this day onwards, always sat on a lower seat and slept on the floor out of respect to the *Adi Granth*.

A special room was prepared for the *Adi Granth* where it would stay overnight. It was then brought into the main hall in the morning for people to read.

## GURDWARAS

Every gurdwara in the world has the same layout as *Harmandir Sahib*, where the scripture is the central attraction, placed on a raised seat. The congregation sits on the floor as humble Sikhs of the Guru. Every gurdwara also has a special room for the scripture called *Sach Khand*, and a *Granthi* to look after it. Sikhs normally visit the gurdwara twice a day, or as often as they can.

◀ Taking the Sikh scripture to the rest room at Amritsar in the evening. It is carried on a gold carriage by up to eight men.

## Guru Granth Sahib

The *Adi Granth* was read by Sikhs throughout the seventeenth century. In 1706, Guru Gobind Singh revised the *Adi Granth* by adding the hymns of the ninth Guru, Guru Tegh Bahadur. Before passing away (in 1708), Guru Gobind Singh said that there should be no more human Gurus, but that the holy scripture should be the Guru from then onwards. He renamed the *Adi Granth* the *Guru Granth Sahib*, and said it should be the Guru of the Sikhs forever.

For education purposes the *Guru Granth Sahib* is divided into four or six volumes. These volumes do not require a separate room or a throne. ▼

Many Sikhs will visit the gurdwara twice a day to pay their respects to the *Guru Granth Sahib*. They will go for morning prayers and for evening prayers. Some Sikhs keep a much-treasured copy of the *Guru Granth Sahib* at home. No matter what a Sikh wants to do, he or she will seek permission from the *Guru Granth Sahib* first.

## READING THE SCRIPTURE

*Guru Granth Sahib* has 1,430 pages. On special occasions, a continuous reading is undertaken which takes forty-eight hours. Five volunteers take turns of two hours each. This non-stop reading is called *Akhand Path*: 'unbroken reading'. When the complete *Guru Granth Sahib* is read slowly at a person's own pace it is called *Sehaj Path*, or 'slowly read'.

A prayer is said in the presence of the *Guru Granth Sahib* which is then opened at random. The first paragraph on the left-hand side is read. This is called an 'order of the Guru' or a 'guidance of the Guru'.

▲ Five people take it in turns to read during an *Akhand Path*. The nearest reader is holding a special fan called a *Chauri* to show respect for the scripture.

All festivals, naming ceremonies, weddings or thanksgiving prayers will take place in the presence of the *Guru Granth Sahib*.

## *Dasam Granth*

It is said that Guru Gobind Singh was a great poet, but he did not add any of his compositions to the *Guru Granth Sahib*. He wrote many hymns and some are used by *Amritdharj* Sikhs (see page 39) as their daily prayers. To keep the compositions of Guru Gobind Singh original and in safe hands they were written down in another book. It was named *Dasam Granth* meaning a 'book of the tenth Guru'. The Sikhs respect the *Dasam Granth*, but the *Guru Granth Sahib* is more important, as declared by Guru Gobind Singh.

# The Sikhs' Sacred Places

There are many different places that are revered by Sikhs in both India and Pakistan. The first four of these, described below, mark events in Guru Nanak's life.

▲ Gurdwara *Janamasthan*, built at the birthplace of Guru Nanak. It has 300 rooms so that visitors can stay overnight.

## Gurdwara *Janamasthan*

This gurdwara marks the birthplace of Guru Nanak in Nankana Sahib. The present building was built with the approval of Emperor Ranjit Singh in 1819–20. It is located on a huge estate of thousands of hectares. Many Sikhs visit this gurdwara on Guru Nanak's birthday.

## Gurdwara *Patti Sahib*

This sacred shrine reminds the Sikhs of Guru Nanak's school days. The Guru was sent here to study with many learned men, to learn the languages of Sanskrit, and then Arabic and Persian at the age of thirteen. His worldly tutors had to bow their heads before the Guru's brilliant mental powers, spiritual knowledge and broad mind. The Guru composed a hymn called *Patti* at this place.

This gurdwara is also visited by Sikhs when they come to Nankana Sahib.

## Gurdwara *Sacha Sauda*

This gurdwara was built on the site where Guru Nanak fed the hungry monks. The spacious, fort-like building was built by Emperor Ranjit Singh. The Sikh congregation of the UK has helped with repairs to this building. It has many rooms for visiting pilgrims to stay in and an *Akhand Path* (see page 29) is recited four times a year here.

## Gurdwara *Kartar Pur Sahib*

This shrine, in Kartarpur by the River Ravi, is an historical place for the Sikhs. It is where Guru Nanak departed from the world. The Maharaja (prince) of Patiala constructed the present building. It was repaired in 1995 by the Pakistan government. It is spacious and beautiful although its location, surrounded by forest and next to the river, makes it hard to maintain.

▲ Gurdwara *Sacha Sauda* was shut for nearly fifty years, after the separation of India and Pakistan in 1947. Now it has been repaired and is open to visitors.

## Harmandir Sahib

This is the most important shrine for Sikhs. Built in the town of Amritsar by Guru Arjan, it is located in the middle of a sacred pool, with a bridge linking it to the land. The foundation stone was laid in CE 1588 and the *Adi Granth* was installed here in 1604.

In 1803, Emperor Ranjit Singh donated a large amount of gold for the dome and roof. Ever since, *Harmandir Sahib* has been known as the Golden Temple. Every Sikh longs to visit this shrine at least once in his or her lifetime, especially on the anniversary of the *Adi Granth* installation day. Many people go to bathe in the sacred pool, believing that it will take away their sins.

## Akal Takhat

Directly opposite *Harmandir Sahib* is another important building, the *Akal Takhat. Akal* means 'God; and *Takhat* means 'seat of authority', so this building is the 'Seat of God'. Guru Har Gobind, the sixth Guru, built this shrine in 1609. Any laws to do with Sikhism are issued from here, making it the highest seat of authority for Sikhs all over the world.

The Golden Temple is surrounded by a complex of many buildings and shrines. The tall building with a clock is one of the four entrances. ▼

## Gurdwara *Sis Ganj*

This gurdwara is in Delhi, the capital of India. It stands on the site where the ninth Guru, Guru Tegh Bahadur, laid down his life for freedom of speech and freedom of worship. A well which supplied the water for the last bath of the Guru's life is still present in the cellar of the gurdwara building. Both Sikhs and non-Sikhs come here regularly to pay respect to and thank the Guru.

## Gurdwara *Bangla Sahib*

This gurdwara stands on the site where the eighth Guru, Guru Har Krishan, stayed during his time in Delhi. Here he cured many sufferers of smallpox. He finally fell prey to the disease himself and passed away at the age of eight. The building of the gurdwara also runs a free hospital, which is open to all.

▲ *Bangla Sahib* Gurdwara, where Sikhs gather to pay respect to the eighth Guru and seek his blessings.

## Takhat Sri Patna Sahib

This gurdwara is in the city of Patna in the state of Bihar, India. The shrine was built to commemorate the birth of Guru Gobind Singh. It is revered as the second *Takhat* of the Sikhs after the *Akal Takhat*.

## Takhat Sri Kesgarh Sahib

This is the place where Guru Gobind Singh created the Khalsa (see page 39). This place symbolizes the turning point in Sikh history. It is revered as the third *Takhat* of the Sikhs. This shrine is second only to *Harmandir Sahib*, as being a shrine a Sikh must visit once in his or her life.

## Takhat Sri Dam Dama Sahib

This gurdwara is in the village of Sabo Ki Talwandi and it is revered as the fourth *Takhat* of the Sikhs. Guru Gobind Singh rested here for almost a year, when he was on his way to the south of India. In 1706 Guru Gobind Singh

▲ The inside of *Sri Patna Sahib*. Here are three copies of the *Guru Granth Sahib*, and a Sikh is serving *Karah Parshad* which is a special sweet pudding served to people during or after the congregation.

revised the *Adi Granth* at this place. Baba Deep Singh, who was the first *Jathedar* (leader) of *Dam Dama Sahib*, made four copies of the *Adi Granth*. This place is also known as *Dam Damai Taksal* which means a school. All Sikh literature produced here is known to be the most authentic.

## Takhat Sri Hazur Sahib

Guru Gobind Singh baptized a monk known as Mado Dass and renamed him as Banda Singh Bahadur. Banda Singh Bahadur was instructed by the Guru to go back to the Punjab and tell the rulers that the Sikhs were not finished, that they were coming back to take what belonged to them. It was at this place, in 1708, that the Guru renamed the *Adi Granth* and declared it to be the *Guru Granth Sahib*. Later that year, Guru Gobind Singh breathed his last. This place is revered as the fifth *Takhat* of the Sikhs.

◀ The present-day Takhat *Dam Dama Sahib*. Dam Dama means 'a place where the Guru rested for a while'.

# Festivals and Special Occasions

Sikh festivals are divided into two categories: Gurpurbs, celebrations related to the Gurus, and Jorhmela, gatherings and fairs.

## Gurpurbs

In India, all *Gurpurbs* are celebrated with great vigour but in Western countries, due to lack of time and official holidays, the only *Gurpurbs* celebrated are Guru Nanak's birthday, Guru Gobind Singh's birthday, Guru Arjan's martyrdom, Guru Tegh Bahadur's martyrdom and the installation day of the *Adi Granth*. The vast majority of gurdwaras will celebrate the *Gurpurb* on the day the festival falls, but some may choose the following weekend so that more people can join in the celebration.

Preparing *Langar* at a gurdwara. A group of women are making flat breads, called chapattis. ▼

In the gurdwara, the celebrations start three days before the event. An *Akhand Path* of the *Guru Granth Sahib* will start at the gurdwara. Many Sikhs will participate in reading the *Guru Granth Sahib*, preparing *Langar*, serving food and many more activities in the gurdwara.

*Bhog*, the completion of the *Akhand Path*, takes place on the third day. Sikhs come to the gurdwara, listen to the reading and join in the singing of praise to God. The preachers tell the history of the event. Prayers are said, to thank the *Guru Granth Sahib* for its guidance. People join in with *Langar* and wish everyone well.

Some gurdwaras have an evening congregation as well. In this session, people sing poems and read poetry. Also, some gurdwaras organize a religious procession through the town during which the *Guru Granth Sahib* leads the way, while the congregation follows chanting hymns. At home, Sikhs will get up early, have a bath and wear new colourful clothes. Some families exchange gifts and visit other family members or friends. There may be a feast of specially prepared food, which continues throughout the day.

In most countries where Sikhs live, Guru Arjan's martyrdom falls in June and the weather can be very hot. Many Sikhs will have stalls serving cold drinks free of charge.

▲ Khalsa Sikhs (see page 39) form a procession to celebrate Guru Nanak's birthday at Anandpur, India.

## THE MAIN GURPURBS

The Sikh calendar is based on the cycles of the moon, while the Western calendar is based on the sun. As lunar months are shorter than solar months, the Sikh calendar is eleven days shorter than the solar calendar. Therefore, each year, most Sikh festivals fall on different days of the Western calendar.

Guru Nanak's birthday falls in October/November
Guru Gobind Singh's birthday falls in December/January
*Guru Granth Sahib* inauguration day falls in August/September
Guru Arjan's martyrdom day falls in June
Guru Tegh Bahadur's martyrdom falls in November.

▲ A *Baisakhi* celebration with Punjabi dancers in the UK.

# Jorhmela

## Baisakhi

This always falls on the Western dates of 13 and 14 April, but in India it is the first day of the month called *Baisakh*. It is the spring harvest festival of north-west India. In fact all Punjabis, of any religion, celebrate it. This festival was celebrated well before Guru Nanak's time. Once farmers had sold their crops they would enjoy themselves at *melas* (funfairs) or visit friends and relatives. Guru Gobind Singh used this day to form the Khalsa Brotherhood.

## Divali

Known as the festival of light, this falls in October or November, and is celebrated by both Sikhs and Hindus. Sikhs celebrate Divali because it brings them the message of freedom and justice. On this day, Sikhs remember their sixth Guru, Guru Har Gobind, who came to Amritsar after his release from Gwalior Jail. He had been kept there for almost two years for not paying the unjust tax called *jazia*.

The Guru's arrival in Amritsar was celebrated by lighting up *Harmandir Sahib* and the people's homes. Today, gurdwaras and houses are decorated with rows of lights and candles, and there are often bonfires and firework displays.

## Hola Mohalla

In 1680, Guru Gobind Singh asked his Sikhs not to celebrate the Hindu festival of Holi, but introduced a new festival called *Hola Mohalla*, meaning 'attack' and 'the place of attack'. Because the Sikhs were being persecuted at that time, the Guru trained them in martial arts and military exercises. Hence *Hola* became a national sports day of the Sikhs. On this day Sikhs all over the world hold tournaments and athletic events.

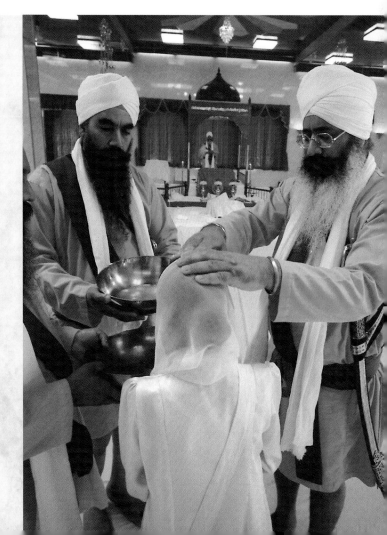

A woman is initiated into the Khalsa by taking *amrit*, a holy liquid made from sugar and water. ▼

### THE KHALSA BROTHERHOOD

On the *Baisakhi* of 1699, the tenth Guru, Guru Gobind Singh created the Khalsa Brotherhood. At this time the Sikhs were being persecuted, and the Guru decided that they needed to form a group of fighters who could defend their faith. He initiated five Sikhs who were prepared to die for what they believed, and called them *panj piare* ('five beloved ones'). They were given five symbols to wear: *kesh* (uncut hair), *kangha* (wooden comb), *kara* (steel bracelet), *kirpan* (sword) and *kachera* (knee-length shorts). These are known as the five Ks. The Khalsa Brotherhood continues to this day. Sikhs who have been initiated are called *amritdharj* because during the ceremony they have taken *amrit*, a holy liquid.

## Birth and naming

There is no birth ceremony in Sikhism. But many Sikhs like to whisper the word *Waheguru* in the ears of the newly born. *Waheguru* means 'wonderful Lord', and is a Sikh name for God. When both mother and child are fit and well a *Granthi* is invited to the home. He or she prepares holy water by reading some hymns and stirring water at the same time. This water is then offered to the mother and a few drops are given to the child.

▲ A baby-naming ceremony in a gurdwara. The baby's mother is accepting holy water from the *Granthi*.

The family, along with the newborn baby, go to the gurdwara for thanksgiving. After prayers requesting a name for the baby, the *Guru Granth Sahib* is opened at random. The first letter of the first word is selected and offered to the family to choose a name for the baby. Once the family has decided, it is declared to the congregation.

## Marriage

Sikhs are encouraged to marry, and marriage is called *Anand Karj*, which means 'the ceremony of bliss'. The Gurus taught that family life was

### SIKH NAMES

A Sikh first name can be used for both men and women. The second name for males is Singh, which means 'lion', and for females is Kaur, which means 'princess'. If Pritam is the first name chosen, Pritam Singh is used for a male and Pritam Kaur is the female name. If Panesar is the surname, then the names would be Pritam Singh Panesar and Pritam Kaur Panesar.

very important. Many Sikh weddings are assisted marriages, where the partners are chosen by the parents, with the partners' consent. Even if the couple have suggested their own marriage, the families will still be very involved.

The most important part of the wedding is the reading of the *Lavan*, a hymn written for weddings by Guru Ram Dass. It has four verses, which are spoken one at a time and then sung. Each verse explains a stage of life.

As each verse is sung, the bride and the groom walk in a clockwise direction around the *Guru Granth Sahib* four times. Everyone joins in the final prayers of the ceremony and the couple are declared man and wife. The ceremony is concluded by distributing the *Karah Parshad*, the blessed food, among the congregation.

▲ Marriage and families are central to the Sikh way of life.

A couple who are being married bow in front of the *Guru Granth Sahib* to accept the wedding vows. ▼

## Death

Guru Nanak explained to his disciples that death is a normal part of a life cycle. We have come, he said, into this world with the date, time and place of death already written. Why then should we worry about death? A quote from the *Guru Granth Sahib* says: 'death, from which this world is afraid, brings joy to me. Because by dying, I can merge with God.'

## Funerals

When a Sikh dies a hymn called *Kirtan Sohila* is recited. In Western countries the body is then taken away by a funeral director. The family will arrange the recitation of the *Guru Granth Sahib* at home or at the gurdwara. A date for the funeral is fixed. Meanwhile, relatives and friends visit the family to convey their sympathy and offer support.

On the day of a funeral, people file past the coffin at home, paying their final respects. A picture of Guru Nanak and Guru Gobind Singh hangs on the wall behind. ▼

On the day of the funeral the body is washed, clothed and brought home so that all the family can see their loved one for the last time. During this visit some hymns are sung.

Since often there isn't enough room in a house, the body is then taken to the gurdwara. Here friends and the members of the congregation can pay their respects by joining in with the recitation of hymns. Although there are no fixed instructions in Sikh laws, the Sikhs prefer to cremate their dead. After the prayer, the body is taken to a crematorium where the *Kirtan Sohila* is chanted again and the last prayers are said. After cremation people will come back to listen to *Bhog* and join in the final prayer. *Langar* is served by the family.

In India, the cremation will take place straight away. The recitation of the *Guru Granth Sahib* starts after the cremation. The date of *Bhog* could be either nine or eleven days later.

## LIFE AFTER DEATH

Sikhs believe in the transmigration of the soul: that a person's soul passes into a different body after death. There are approximately 8.4 million species on this earth. Of these, 4.2 million live on land and 4.2 million live in water. Sikhs believe a soul can travel through any one of them, and that human form is the final form. A person has the ability to think and can achieve union with God through his or her actions. One can come out of the cycle of birth and death, if one lives life in accordance with God's instructions.

Prayers are offered at a gurdwara, before the body is taken away for cremation. ▶

# Sikhism Today

In the past, Sikhs suffered persecution from various groups. Today, however, they can be seen in every walk of life.

▲ A Sikh family in New York. Some devout Sikh women also wear turbans.

Two Gurus, Guru Gobind Singh's four children and millions of Sikhs sacrificed their lives for their religion. To survive, Sikhs became the best-known warriors in India. But now the Sikh homeland, Punjab, is the richest and most prosperous part of India. Sikhs have adapted well to modern technology and are successful people.

## Sikhs around the world

Many Sikhs have moved to a variety of countries. With their friendly nature and ability to work hard they have earned the respect of many people. In the USA alone there are almost 200,000 Sikh converts. Even so, while settling in foreign countries, Sikhs sometimes faced discrimination due to their dress code and religious beliefs. Wherever Sikhs move, they take with them not only the Gurus' teaching but also the *Guru Granth Sahib* itself. They build gurdwaras to hold daily congregations and to be near their Guru.

## Three groups

Sikhs of the twenty-first century can be divided into three basic groups. These are:

1 *Sahajdhari*: A Sikh who believes in the Sikh code of conduct but does not wear a turban. Men are clean shaven.

2 *Kesadhari*: Wears the turban and beard, but is not ready to take *Amrit*.

3 *Amritdhari*: A Sikh who has taken *Amrit* and wears the five Ks.

They all strongly believe in Guru Nanak's teachings and fully support their faith.

## Challenges today

Sikhs have a tradition of being strong and brave and have stood up to many challenges. Today their struggle is against what they see as the enemy of humanity: the permissive society. They see people's lives, especially the young, being devalued by fashion, media and drugs. There are many organizations for young Sikhs, working constantly to teach them the values of Sikhism. There are many positive results but there is still a long way to go. However, Sikhs believe in self-help and are always optimistic by nature.

It is evident that the teaching of Guru Nanak has developed the Sikhs into hardworking people who respect freedom and equality, and stand against oppression.

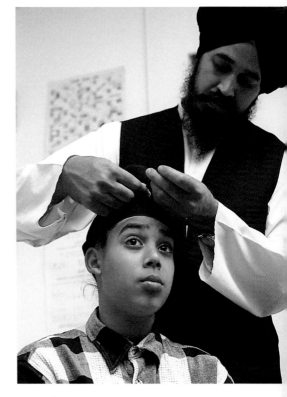

▲ A father helps his son to tie his turban.

Young Sikhs outside a gurdwara in the UK. ▼

# Glossary

*Adi Granth* The first Sikh holy book, compiled in 1604 by Guru Arjan.

*Akhand Path* Continuous reading of the *Guru Granth Sahib*, from beginning to end.

*Amrit* Holy liquid made from sugar and water, used in Khalsa initiation ceremonies.

*Amritdharj* Someone who has 'taken' *Amrit*, and who has joined the Khalsa Brotherhood.

**Astrologer** A person who studies the movements and positions of stars and planets, and who predicts how these will have an effect on people and their lives.

*Bhog* The end of the *Akhand Path*, the long reading of the *Guru Granth Sahib*.

**Castes** Classes or divisions in Hindu society.

**Compile** Make a collection by putting together things from different places.

**Congregation** A group of people who have come together for religious worship.

**Disciples** Followers or pupils of a teacher or leader.

**Five Ks** Five symbols worn by Sikhs who have been initiated into the Khalsa Brotherhood; who are *amritdharj*.

*Granthi* Reader of the *Guru Granth Sahib*, who conducts ceremonies.

**Gurdwara** Sikh place of worship. Means 'doorway to the Guru'.

**Guru** Enlightener. In Sikhism, the title of Guru is reserved for the ten human Gurus and the *Guru Granth Sahib*.

*Guru Granth Sahib* Sikh scriptures, initially compiled by Guru Arjan and given its final form by Guru Gobind Singh.

**Holy** Belonging to God, sacred.

**Hymn** A religious song of praise.

**Impostors** People who pretend to be someone they are not, in order to deceive other people.

**Initiated** Allowed, with a formal ceremony, into a society or group.

*Jazia* A tax that had to be paid by non-Muslims in India if they wanted to observe their own religion.

**Khalsa** The (Sikh) community of the pure.

*Langar* Guru's kitchen. The gurdwara dining hall and the food served in it.

**Martyrdom** The death of someone who has been killed because of his or her religious beliefs.

*Moguls* Muslim people who originally came from Mongolia. They ruled much of India from the sixteenth to nineteenth centuries.

*Mool Mantar* Basic teaching; essential teaching. The basic statement of belief at the beginning of the *Guru Granth Sahib*.

**Persecuted** Treated very badly for a long time.

**Punjab** Land of five rivers. The area of India in which Sikhism originated.

**Punjabi** The language of the Punjab. Also, a person who lives in or comes from the Punjab.

**Sacred** Connected to God; holy.

**Salvation** Escape from sin and its results.

**Scriptures** Sacred writings of a religion.

**Sikh** Learner; disciple. A person who believes in the ten Gurus and the *Guru Granth Sahib*, and who has no other religion.

**Shrine** A holy place, sometimes containing a religious statue.

**Soul** The spiritual part of a person, which may live for ever.

*Takhat* Seat of authority.

**Varna system** A Hindu system of dividing all people into groups. These groups are based on a person's inborn qualities, and the work associated with them.

# Further Information

## Books to read

*Discovering Religions: Sikhism* by Sue Penney
(Heinemann, 1996)
*I Am a Sikh* by M. Aggarwal (Franklin Watts, 2001)
*Listening to Sikhs* by Oliva Bennett (Collins
Educational, 1990)
*Religions of the World: Sikhism* by D. Singh and
A. Smith (Hodder Wayland, 2001)
*Sikh Temples (Places of Worship)* by Kanwaljit
Kaur-Singh (Heinemann, 1999)
*What Do We Know About Sikhism?* by Beryl
Dhanjal (Hodder Wayland, 1996)

## Web pages

http://www.sikhnet.com
A comprehensive website of Sikh information,
history, community contacts, youth, music,
shopping, etc. Many links to other Sikh websites.
Detailed listing of gurdwaras all over the world.

http://www.srigurugranthsahib.org
Concentrates on the spiritual side of the religion.
Contains audio clips of scripture readings.

http://www.allaboutsikhs.com
Information on the Gurus, scripture, history,
gurdwaras and youth issues.

## Place to visit

Anyone can visit a gurdwara during the
congregation, but if a guided tour is required prior
arrangements should be made. For a list of
gurdwaras around the world visit
www.sikhnet.com (see above).

Victoria & Albert Museum
Cromwell Road, London SW7 2RL
Tel: 0207 942 2000
Has an Indian collection containing some Sikh items.

## Other media resources

BBC Education produces schools media resources
on different faiths.
BBC Information
PO Box 1116, Belfast BT2 7AJ
Tel: 08700 100 222
email: info@bbc.co.uk
http://www.bbc.co.uk/schools

Channel 4 produces schools media resources on
different faiths, including Animated World Faiths.
C4 Schools
PO Box 100, Warwick CV34 6TZ
Tel: 01926 436444
email:sales@schools.channel4.co.uk
http://www.channel4.com/schools

## For further information, books and resources

The Institute of Indian Art and Culture
The Bhavan Centre, 4a Castletown Road
West Kensington, London W14 9HQ
Tel: 0207 381 3045

The Commonwealth Institute Resource Centre
Kensington High Street, London W8 6NQ
Tel: 0207 603 4535
http://www.commonwealth.org.uk

The Sikh Missionary Society
10 Featherstone Road, Southall, Middx UB2 5AA
Tel: 0208 574 1902
Fax: 0208 8574 1912

DTF (the book and artefact shop)
117 Soho Road, Handsworth, Birmingham  B21
Tel: 0121 515 1183

# Index

The numbers in **bold** refer to photographs and maps, as well as text.

*Adi Granth* 22, **24**–7, 28, 32, 35, 36, 46
Akal Takhat 32, 34
*Akhand Path* **29**, 31, 36, 37, 46
*Amrit* 39, 45, 46
*Amritdharj* 29, 39, 46
Amritsar 7, **19**, 23, 24, 25, 26–7, 32, 38, 39
Anandpur 7, **37**
astrologer 7, 46

*Baisakhi* **38**, 39
Benares 7, 9
Bhag Kaur **17**
Bhai Gurdass 7, 24
*Bhog* 37, 43, 46

castes 7, 46
*Chauri* **24**, 27, **29**
congregation 22, 27, 31, 34, 37, 40, 41, 43, 44, 46
cremation 12, 13, 43

*Dasam Granth* 29
death 14, 42–3, 46
Delhi 7, 33
disciples 4, 7, 12, 42, 46
Divali 38–9

Eminabad 7, 10
equality 4, 16, 17, 18, 25, 45

family **5**, 8, 17, 20, **21**, 37, 40, **41**, 42, 43, **44**
festivals 29, 36–9
five evils 15, **23**
five Ks 39, 45, 46
funerals 17, 42–3

God 4, 5, 6, 7, 9, 11, 14, 15, 19, 20, 21, 23, 25, 32, 37, 40, 42, 43, 46
Golden Temple see *Harmandir Sahib*
*Granthi* 27, **40**, 46
gurdwaras 5, 16, 19, 24, 26, 27, 28, 34, 36, 37, 39, **40**, 42, 43, 44, 45, 46
  *Bangla Sahib* **33**
  *Janamasthan* **30**
  *Kartar Pur Sahib* 31
  *Patti Sahib* 30
  *Sacha Sauda* **31**
  *Sis Ganj* 33
Gurmukhi **25**, 26
*Gurpurbs* 36–7

*Guru Granth Sahib* 4, 5, 11, 13, **16**, 19, 21, 22, 23, **25**, **28–9**, **34**, 35, 36, 37, 40, 41, 42, 43, 44, 46
Gurus 4, 5, 9, 12, **13**, 16, 18, 21, 22, 23, 24, 25, 36, 40, 44, 46
  Amar Dass **13**, 17, 22
  Angad **12**, **13**, 16, 22
  Arjan **13**, **22**, **23**, **24**, 25, 26, 27, 32, 46
    martyrdom 36, 37
  Guru Gobind Singh **13**, 17, 20, 28, 29, 34, 35, 36, 38–9, 42, 44, 46
    birthday 36, 37
  Guru Nanak 4, 5, **6–13**, 14, 15, 16, 17, 18, 19, 20, 21, 22, **23**, 25, 26, 30–31, 38, 42, 45,
    birthday 6–7, 30, 36, **37**
    death 12–13
    journeys 9, 10, 12
  Guru Har Gobind **13**, 32, 38
  Guru Har Krishan **13**, 33
  Guru Har Rai **13**
  Guru Ram Dass **13**, 22, 41
  Guru Tegh Bahadur **13**, 28, 33,
    martyrdom 37
Gwalior 7, 38

*Harmandir Sahib* 24, **26–7**, **32–3**, 34, 39
Hindus 4, 5, 12, 19, 38, 39, 46
*Hola Mohalla* 39
hymns 5, 7, 22, 23, 24–5, 28, 29, 30, 37, 40, 41, 43, 46

*Ik Onkar* 4
India 4, **7**, 9, 16, 19, 20, 30, 31, 32, 34, 36, 37, 38, 43, 44, 46
initiation 39, 46

*jazia* 18, 38, 46
*Jorhmela* 36, 38–9

Kalu, Mheta 6, 7, 8, 9
Kartarpur 7, 12, 31
Khalsa 34, **37**, 38, **39**, 46
*Khanda* 5
*Karah Parshad* 34, 41

Lahore 7, 25
Lalo **10**
*Langar* 5, **19**, **36**, 37, 43, 46
laws 17, 21, 32, 43

Malik Bhago 10–11
marriage 17, 21, 40–**41**
martyrdom 36, 37, 46
meditation 5, 14, 20
Moguls 18, 46
monks 8, 9, 21, 31, 35
*Mool Mantar* 4, 9, 46
Muslims 4, 5, 12, 18, 19, 25, 46

naming 29, 40
Nanaki 6, 7, 9
Nankana Sahib 7, **30**

Pakistan 7, 30, 31
Patna 7, 34
persecution 39, 46
*Pothi* 22, 23, 24
prayer 4, 12, 14, 28, 29, 37, 40, 41, 43
Punjab 4, 7, 35, 44, 46
Punjabi 4, 26, **38**, 46

Sabo Ki Talwandi 7, 34
sacred places 30–35
salvation 5, 21, 46
scripture 4, 22–29, 46
*sewa* 5, **14**
shrine 12, 26, 30, 31, 32, 34, 46
Sikhism 4–5, 13, 16, 18, 25, 32, 39, 40, 42, 44–5, 46
Sikhs 4, 5, 7, 12, 13, 14, 15, 17, 18, 19, 21, 22, 23, 26. 27, 28, 29, 30, 31, 32, 33, 34, 35, 36, 37, 39, 40, 41, 43, 44, 45, 46
souls 14, 43, 46
Sultanpur 7, **9**

*Takhat* 34–5, 46
  *Sri Dam Dama Sahib* 34–35
  *Sri Hazur Sahib* 35
  *Sri Kesgarh Sahib* 34
  *Sri Patna Sahib* **34**
transmigration 14, 43
turbans 18, **44**, **45**

UK 31, **38**, **45**
USA 44

Varna system 4, 46

women **16–17**, 18, **36**, **39**, 40, **44**